Dow
Handboo

A Pocket Resource for Building Arrows
with Wooden Dowels

LEVI DREAM PUBLISHING

Published by Levi Dream, 2011

Levi Dream Publishing, P.O. Box 75203, Honolulu, HI 96836-0203

Printed in the U.S.A., Charleston, SC

First Printing in 2011

ISBN: 978-0-9832481-2-5

Library of Congress Cataloging-in-Publication Data is available
on file.

For Levi, my Little Arrow

Angela, my Life Companion

God, my Guiding Light

One of my first sets of dowel arrows. I have all five original arrows. The second one from the top ended up skimming a target stand and hitting a light pole. The steel tip was smashed and the feathers sheared off. With a new tip and new feathers, this arrow has performed faithfully since.

I would take a well-made dowel arrow over a factory wood arrow any day.

Table of Contents

Preface

There are many reasons why I would write a book about dowel arrows. Though of all those reasons, the number one is because I care about your safety and well-being. I have heard so many stories of people being admitted to the hospital because they got a splintered dowel shaft slammed through their arm. I have personally seen what a hastily-made and poorly-planned dowel arrow can do when shot. I myself have had many nearly-irreparable injuries due to dowel shafts.

Every time I go to an archery range or somewhere with my archery tackle, I always hear the same thing.

"Those are some really nice arrows you've got. What are they made of? Not dowel rods, are they? You could hurt somebody. You're not actually SHOOTING them, are you?"

And honestly, I can't blame them. Too many people have seen or experienced the damage 'cheap' arrows can do. Arrows shouldn't be cheap, and when done right, are never cheap. A good arrow either takes your time or your money, and in the end, that's how it should be.

Now that I've scared you, I will explain myself. You are probably thinking, "Man, I bought this book so I could make some cheap arrows and this guy says he won't do it, what a rip-off!" Don't worry, I will show you how to make arrows with dowels. But it will take time to do it right, and really, your life and comfort is worth it.

Back to me, I originally didn't want to make arrows. My first bow was my dad's 45 pound fiberglass recurve, and my very first arrow was a dowel rod with a notch on one end, a point sanded onto the other, and duct tape for vanes. I had cut the notch too shallow, and the arrow just slipped off the string when I fired it, falling uselessly to the ground.

Looking back, I was very lucky. Chances are if the arrow had flown, it would have blown apart, probably ending up in my arm, hand, or face. It would have prematurely ended my archery career. That would have been no fun at all.

After that failed attempt, I looked up how to make arrows that worked. After finding a picture of what a wooden shaft can do if it breaks, I decided to go modern and bought all my arrows. Eventually I moved to carbon shafting, which became my personal favorite until I saw one break. I looked it up and found some pictures.

Imagine thousands of razor splinters of carbon embedded in a person's hand, all of which are spread out on the exit end, making the wound that much more horrendous. After that, a few splinters of wood didn't seem so bad.

So I went and bought myself some wooden arrows. They were made of Port Orford Cedar, spined for my 45 pound guava selfbow, and cost almost $8 a piece, not counting shipping to my island state of Hawaii. At that price, they were even more expensive than my carbon arrows, but I didn't care. I paid the high price because I wanted quality, and didn't want to go through the carbon explosion experience.

Despite my high expectations, they didn't last long. Most started cracking and needed to be trashed after a hundred shots or so, some simply snapped at the target, and one exploded. Needless to say, I was quite dissapointed, and my wife wasn't liking the amount of money I was spending on bad arrows.

After some research and applying some of my experience making bows, I bought some cedar shafts that I got to pick through myself. After some poor fletching, I had somewhat innacurate but durable arrows. With that bolstering my arrow-making bravery, I made more, and got better at fletching.

That's when I started getting back into dowels. I tried picking through them like the cedar shafts, but honestly, after looking at over four-hundred dowels, I got lazy. I had a couple nice ones, and the rest were picked because they were straight. I still have a couple with me today, and ten near-injuries.

After that, I realized that like lumber bows, there was no room for laziness. There was no forgiveness. The smallest flaw and you could have lethal consequences. With a renewed determination, I bought more dowels. This time, I only got five out of a box of 500 that would do.

I still have all five arrows, despite having them hit target stands or being speared by other arrows. They survived. Since then, all of my target shafts are dowels. I also hand-plane arrows, but that's a different book. It has been my experience that a well-made and well-tuned

dowel arrow will outlast any commerical wooden shaft
and perform just as well if not better.

That is a bold statement, and a far-cry from the
'uselessness' of dowels for shafting. I am not saying that
any dowel will make a good arrow. In fact, almost all
dowels made for industy or hobby/crafts will not make
good arrows, nor were they designed for that purpose. But
like in anything, there are exceptions.

If I haven't scared you out of using dowels yet,
(hopefully I have scared you out of using carbon shafts if
shooting off the hand) then continue onward. You are the
reason I am writing this book, so thank you and God bless.

Chapter 1
Arrow Shafts

Welcome to the Dowel Arrow Handbook! In this Chapter, we will go over everything involved in selecting and preparing arrow shafts from dowels. There will be some general arrow theory including spine and the archer's paradox.

We will also go over the very important task of inspecting dowels. You will learn what to look for as far as grain and growth rings are concerned, and how to weed out any potentially dangerous arrow shafts.

And finally, we will go over how to straighten shafts by hand and how to crest and finish your arrow shafts.

Diameter, Spine, Arrow-Tuning

One of the first decisions you will make in arrow-making is how the arrow works in relation to the bow it is fired from. If you are making arrows for multiple bows, then all you need is an approximation of what will be discussed in this section. If you want to get the most out of the symbiotic relationship known as the bow and arrow, continue on.

Every bow is different and unique, regardless of how precision the equipment or skilled the bowyer. Like you or I, each bow will vary slightly, making a one-size fits all approach to arrows (which is how most commercial arrows are produced) not as effective as matching each arrow to the bow it is fired from. A good bow can fire any arrow reasonably well, but a matched arrow will bring any bow to a new level of accuracy and efficiency.

When making arrows, one important factor is known as spine. Simply put, spine is the stiffness of an arrow. Not so simply put, spine is also the ability for an arrow to recover during flight, as well as its ability to withstand the forces of flex that are imparted to it every time it is fired.

One of the easiest ways to estimate spine is by choosing your starting shaft diameter. Dowels come in a wide-variety of diameters, but the basic four for arrows is $\frac{5}{16}''$, $\frac{3}{8}''$, $\frac{7}{16}''$, and $\frac{1}{2}''$. $\frac{5}{16}''$ dowels usually spine anywhere from 30-55 pounds, $\frac{3}{8}''$ range from 60-80 pounds, $\frac{7}{16}''$

range from about 90-110 pounds, and $^1/_2$ works for anything over 120 pounds.

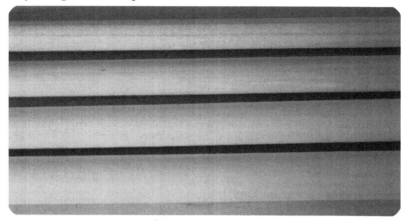

In this picture above, the dowels from top to bottom are $^5/_{16}''$, $^3/_8''$, $^7/_{16}''$, and $^1/_2''$. This is to give you a good idea of size differences. For most bows, $^5/_{16}''$ and $^3/_8''$ dowels are large enough.

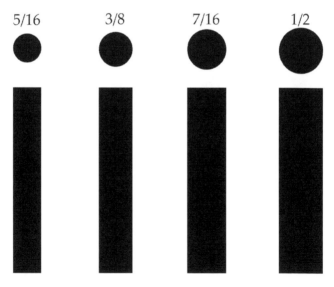

Arrow Shafts

The little chart on the opposite page is a good guide when looking at dowels. This chart is to-scale and is a great way to find out what diameter of dowel you have if they aren't marked. If buying from most hardware stores, dowels are usually color-coded red, blue, green, and gray. These correspond to $5/_{16}''$, $3/_8''$, $7/16''$, and $1/_2''$ respectively. This may vary from store to store, so don't rely on color exclusively.

When dealing with diameter and spine, the weights given are for modern longbows and recurves at 28 inches. For compounds, (yes, you can use wood arrows in a compound, but it has to be a perfect shaft with no flaws) take away fifteen pounds. So for $5/_{16}''$, it will be from 15-40 pounds. For self-bows and older backed longbows, add five pounds, so a $5/_{16}''$ dowel will fit a 40-60 pound bow.

Length also plays a role in the diameter of shaft you choose. The weights given above are for a 28 inch draw, or a 30 inch arrow. To find your approximate draw length, you can take your wingspan (measured from the tips of your fingers. You don't actually need to have wings) and divide it by 2.5.

This will give you your average draw length, though depending on how you shoot and where you anchor, this can go up or down a few inches. My favorite way to determine draw length is to draw your bow with a long arrow nocked, to whatever length is comfortable to you, and have somebody mark where the arrow and bow hand meet at the front.

Once you have your draw length, you can figure out

your arrow length. The length of your arrow will change the spine of that arrow. The longer the arrow, the weaker the spine. For $^5/_{16}$", a 30" arrow will have a spine range of 30-55 pounds for modern recurves and longbows. At the same diameter, a 31" arrow will have a spine range from 25-50 pounds. For further example, a 29" arrow will spine at around 35-60 pounds.

Now all of the spine ratings I have given so far are approximate, and I assume you do not have access to a spine-tester. In order to find a more accurate rating, a spine-tester is needed. They can be purchased for around $100, and most archery pro-shops will let you use theirs if you ask nicely.

Spine is important for two reasons. One, it establishes a safe zone for arrows if you are making arrows for non-precise shooting. For example, if your arrow has a spine of 50 pounds at 28 inch draw, it can be used safely in a bow with a draw-weight of 50 pounds or less at 28 inches (35 for compounds).

The second reason is for accuracy. An arrow whose spine with all things considered is matched to a bow will be very accurate, as the arrow will be stiff enough to recover from the flex imparted upon it, but not too weak as to flex wildly and never recover. When testing an arrow, always err on the side of caution. A stiff spine will push the shot off-target, a weak spine may cause the arrow to explode.

The final variable that will affect spine is the weight of the tip of the arrow. Basically, the heavier the point, the weaker your overall spine. So the heavier your point, the higher spined your arrow needs to be to compensate. The reason is that because the bowstring pushes your arrow from the back, the heavier the point, the more the arrow will flex.

Taking all of these variables together, you can fine-tune your arrows. When I am making arrows for a particular bow, I pick a diameter in the range of the bow's weight and length of draw, but don't adjust for tip weight. After marking each arrow so I know which is which, I then test-fire the arrows into a marked target. I aim at the dead-center of the target, shooting every arrow once.

Some will land to the left, some to the right. This variation is part of the archer's paradox. The arrow is constantly flexing once it exits the bow. While not as noticeable in modern recurves and longbows, and almost negligible in compounds, the archer's paradox is most apparent in longbows and selfbows.

When shooting a longbow, the arrow needs to clear the bow itself. If the arrow is properly spined, it will wrap around the bow, flexing back and forth until it hits the target in a direct line from string to target. When shooting a longbow, you should aim straight from the nock of the arrow, through the center of the handle, and to the target.

If you are right handed and shooting mediterranean style, the arrows will go to the left if they are too stiff, to the right if they are too weak. The reason this happens is because a stiff arrow will not fully wrap around the bow, causing it to launch to the side the arrow is placed on the bow. A weak arrow will wrap around the bow too much, causing it to whip around to the right. Reverse all of this for lefties.

If your arrows are too stiff, a light sanding near the center of the arrow can adjust the spine down. Try those arrows again, adjusting accordingly. If the arrows are flying way off to the left, try going down a diameter.

If the arrows are too weak, you can shorten them slightly, grind the tips down or change them out to make them lighter, or just set them aside for a lighter bow. If they are flying way off ot the right, try going up a diameter. If the arrows are weak, any flaws in the wood will be magnified. Firing them too many times will cause them to break.

Once you've established at least one arrow that lines up perfectly, you can do a couple things that will help in sorting out future arrows. If you weigh the arrow, keeping your other arrows in the same weight will bring them near the proper spine. Another option, and one that takes a bit of practice and repetition, is to spine by feel. Hold the arrow in both hands about ten inches apart. Flex the shaft, and remember how it feels. Once you get a feel for it, you can get a good estimate of arrow spines just by feel.

Now that we have an idea of how to choose diameters and how to adjust your shafts to match a bow, let's move on to the fun part: selecting the actual dowels.

Selecting Dowels

The most important part of making dowel arrows is selecting your dowels. It may sound obvious, but this is the part that will take the most time and patience. When most people think of making arrows with dowels, they tend to look for the straightest ones. The assumption is that a straight dowel is straight like an arrow, and so it will be structurally sound like a good arrow should be.

The truth is, a straight dowel has less to do with its structural stability and more to do with how it was milled, how it was dried, how it was stored, what its moisture content is, and how elastic the wood is. Take these two dowels below.

The bottom one is obviously straight. The top one is obviously curved, and pretty badly too. Which one will make a good arrow? The answer: the top one. Here are the same two dowels up close and with the growth rings marked with a pen.

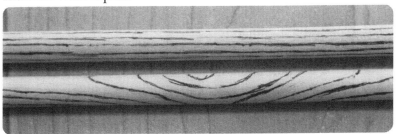

It is clear that the top one, though curved, follows the growth rings closely. The bottom one, though straight, actually has several areas like this one, where the wood was violated. Imagine wood is a bundle of straws. The top dowel is a bent bundle of straight straws, but all the straws are intact.

The bottom dowel is a bundle of bent straws that have been cut down to make them appear straight. What happens is that there are areas where the straws don't even touch each other. It is at places like these where an arrow can easily snap when fired.

The moral of these two dowels is that growth-ring orientation and grain is much more important than straightness. A bent arrow can be straightened, but an arrow on the verge of breaking cannot be saved. It will only be a danger to you and others.

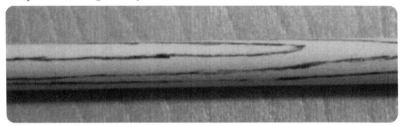

Take a look at the dowel above. this is a reasonable dowel viewed from an angle. You can see where the growth rings lift off from the shaft and dissapear. This is called run-off. When run-off occurs, the overall strength of the shaft is compromised. The more growth rings that can be followed from end to end without run-offs, the better.

It is also important that run-off occurs in only one

direction per side. Take a look at the dowel below.

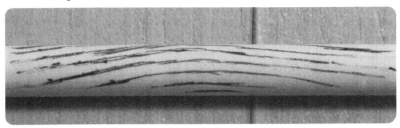

While there is still at least half of the wood intact through this little dip, the dip causes run-offs to occur in two directions. Run-off is dangerous because it can cause the wood to lift a splinter and catch on things. Some of the things it can catch on are the bow, your arm, your hand, and the arrow-rest.

If the wood lifts, it can explode, shear off, or snap. If the run-off is all in one direction, it can be positioned so that the chances of splinters lifting is minimized. That is not possible if the run-off is in two directions.

So what should you look for? Take a look at the dowel above. While not perfect, it is a good compromise. The run-off is minimal, and only goes in one direction. While run-offs are inevitable, it is best to make sure that if there is any run-off, it be at the ends of the arrow. And if there is run-off at the end of an arrow, make that your tip.

Once the arrow is fired, the tip has had no contact with you or the bow. The worst that could happen is it breaks on contact with the target. If the run-off is near the nock end, the nock could shear apart if it is a self-nock, or simply snap if it is glued on. Either way, the nock end has to travel the full length of your draw during flight, and the chances of any splinters linfting is that much higher.

Another thing to looks out for is the grain. If the grain is straight, the sides perpendicualr to the growth rings will appear smooth and clear. Any knots or dips should be avoided. Another thing to avoid is curl or figure. Curl is very beautiful, and will seem to change color like tiger's eye if tilted from left to right. This is caused by the open ends of the grain picking up light differently. This is what curl looks like.

It is very pretty, and in most types of woodwork is a very desirable feature. In an arrow, it should be avoided at all costs. Curly grain should be looked at like run-offs. They can cause the same damage. Make sure that each dowel is clear and free from this type of figure.

Now that you know what to look for as far as grain and growth rings are concerned, the next part to selecting dowels is to know what kind of wood you are dealing with. There are many species of tree that are used to make dowels. Many of them make poor arrows. Considering that dowels weren't manufactured for arrow production, it is lucky that some species are usable.

When buying purpose-made arrow-shafting (which are technically dowels anyway), mostly softwoods are used. These shafts are slected for grain clarity, lack of run off, straight growth-ring orientation, and are straightened. The shafts that make it through are a very tiny percentage of all shafts made. This brings the chances of finding good arrow stock in production dowels (which are made without any real consideration for grain or growth-ring orientation) almost impossible.

While softwoods are famous for use in arrows, they should be avoided in dowel-stock unless a perfect shaft presents itself. Even so, softwood shafts are typically harder to straighten without damaging the shaft, and crack and splinter easier than hardwood shafts.

Most of the time, softwoods are lighter than hardwoods. Most lumber yards and hardware stores will tell you what kind of wood is used in the dowel, or at least if it is a hardwood or not. If made in the US, some common woods for dowels are maple, poplar, cherry, walnut, red and white oak, ash, and birch.

Maple, poplar, and birch appear similar, the wood appearing creamy in color with fine growth rings. Birch may have darker streaks running through it, and poplar may be a light gray or even green. Walnut and cherry have a similar texture, with cherry being more reddish-brown, and walut being more of a grayish-brown. The oaks, as well as ash, have very distinct bands separating the growth rings. Ash and white oak are creamy in color, and red oak is a creamy color to a reddish-brown.

If made overseas, there are many species of wood that are possible. A couple of the more common ones found in hardware stores are ramin, teak, and kwila. Ramin looks very similar to birch, and is one of the better arrow-woods as far as dowels go. If it was made in China, chances are this is that it is.

If the dowel came from Southeast Asia or the Pacific, any number of woods could have been used. The most common are teak and kwila, which both range from a gray color to a deep brown. They also vary in density depending on where in the tree the dowels were cut.

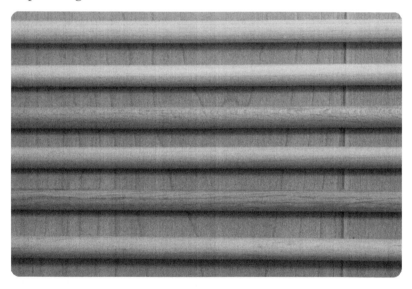

From top to bottom, the woods here are laminated birch, poplar, teak, ramin, red oak, and birch. Be cautious of laminated dowels as they have a tendency to snap without warning. There are places where you can buy laminated shafting, but those are made with better adhesives and controlled for quality. Most of the commercial laminated dowels won't pass the next test.

As far as exotic woods go, most will work as an arrow provided the grain is straight and the wood is sound. Depending on the density of the wood, you can get unusually high spines with thinner shafts. I have an ipe arrow that is only $5/_{16}$″, but spines in the 90's.

Once you've selected some shafts, and you know they are perfect, go ahead and buy them. I do not suggest buying bulk orders of dowels, as most of them (sometimes 99 percent or more) will be tossed. Now comes the final and crucial part of selecting your arrows. This will usually give you a nice, 50-50 split. So if you bought 12 perfect dowels, expect only 6 arrows. More, and you are lucky.

Start by holding the dowel between both hands, about ten inches apart. Make sure this is centered over the center of where you would cut your arrow, as this is the part that takes the most flex when the arrow is fired. Make sure you have a good grip on the dowel.

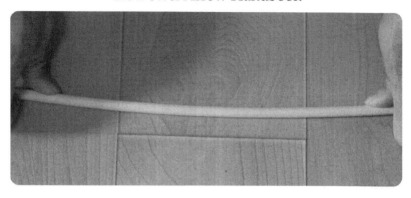

With the dowel held firmy between both hands, flex it about this far. You want the ends of you arrow when cut to be at least an inch away from the center in deflection. This mimics the flex an arrow goes through when fired through a bow. If the dowel makes any sort of cracking or creaking noise, return it. If cracks start to appear, snap it and throw it away. If it simply keeps the bend, place it in a dry place for a couple days and try again.

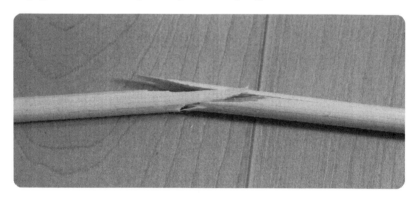

If it snaps, throw it away. Even shafts that look perfect can snap. Better to have it snap now than when it is coming off a bow at anywhere from 80 to 200 miles per hour. Once your shafts have passed every consideration, and this last test a few times, you can now prep the shafts and get them ready for fletching, nocking, and mounting points.

This last flex test should also be done every time you shoot your arrows. A dowel, and wood in general, is very funny. It can hold on for a long time without any problems, and snap for seemingly no reason. Check your arrows before and after every shot.

If an arrow out of your quiver shows signs of cracking, is making noises, or is visibly damaged, snap it in half and salvage the points and fletchings. If an arrow out of the target shows signs of cracking, is making noises, or is visibly damaged, snap it in half and salvage the points and fletchings. Just because you know the arrow you put on the side is unsafe, doesn't mean other people do. I've had a good friend pick up one of my broken arrows and fire it. It exploded.

Never, never leave a questionable shaft intact. Snapping it in half lets anybody know not to use the arrow. And don't assume that somebody else will notice a break even if it is obvious (the tip is hanging off or the arrow is badly bent). Everyone assumes your gear is safe. Don't give them a reason to doubt that.

Now that all that seriousness is out of the way, on to the real fun part! Time to straighten and finish up those arrow shafts!

Straightening

Like I said earlier, it is better to find perfect grain than to find a straight dowel. The chances of finding a perfect shaft is very small, and finding a perfect shaft that is also perfectly straight is really pushing the odds. Searching through hundreds of dowels only to find a few is frustrating enough. A thousand dowels for only a couple shafts? I'd rather learn to straighten.

There are many ways to straighten an arrow, and some methods for pulling even really bad kinks out of wood. Now those techniques are better suited for hand-planing arrows from larger stock (boards, logs, saplings, etc.), and are relatively useless for dowels.

Because of the nature of dowels and the nature of wood in general, if your shafts are indeed perfect with any run-off in only one direction, you shouldn't have very complex bends to correct. For this reason we'll only be using three techniques for straightening arrows.

The first is simple hand-straightening. Unlike softwood arrows like port orford cedar and sitka spruce, hardwood arrows will lose their straightness over time. Sometimes it takes hundreds of shots, sometimes it takes a few minutes in the quiver. For this reason, being able to correct a slightly warped shaft in the field is very important.

The second is by burnishing against the curve. Burnishing the flexed side of a warped shaft will compress the wood in that area, allowing the arrow to straighten out. Burnishing can be done over large curves, but excels at straightening small, tight kinks.

The final method we'll be discussing is using dry heat. When wood is heated, the individual fibers within the wood become slightly loose. This enables the fibers to slide over one another, so that large or stubborn bends can be eased out of the wood. Once cooled, the fibers will set in their new position.

The first way to see if your arrow shaft needs straightening is to take the shaft and sight down its length from the top like in the picture above. Even apparently straight shafts can be warped. If the bend it slight, hand straightening is usually more than enough to fix it. Straightening by hand is great for keeping your arrows straight while shooting. Be sure to inspect and straighten arrows after every shot. After a few times, it becomes very quick and easy to do.

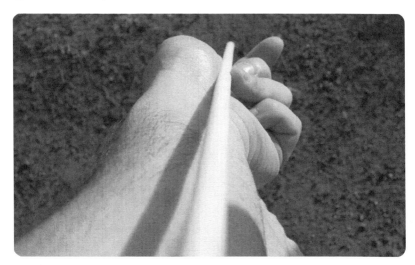

To hand-straighten, start by holding the back of the shaft in your dominant hand, and the bend against the heel of your other palm like in the picture above. Wrap your fingers around the shaft slightly so you can exert force to counter the bend.

Arrow Shafts

Next, use your fingers to pull the arrow into a flex counter to the bend in the shaft. Then slide your hand forward, more or less massaging the dowel.

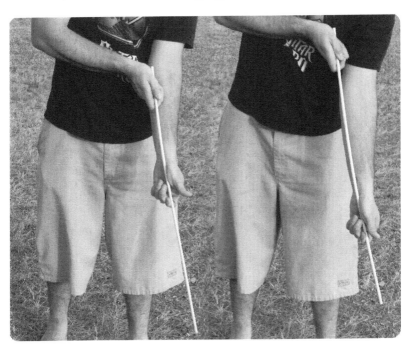

It is easier to see what to do from the front. Me and my evil robo-clone will demonstrate. Start by loosely holding the dowel in your dominant hand, the bent area cupped in your other hand. With a forward sliding motion, exert force while pressing the heel of your palm into the bent area.

When done, check to see if the shaft is straight. The first few times you may need to re-straighten the shaft. It is very easy to push the shaft too hard and bend it in the opposite direction, or in a totally different direction.

the Dowel Arrow Handbook

Straightening by hand may take a few tries to master, but it is well-worth it and is a breeze compared to selecing dowels. When finished, your shaft should now look straight when viewed from the end.

The second method of straightening is best used for shafts that are warped in different directions or are more kinky (not that kind of kinky) than curved. A good example of this is the dowel below.

You can see the curve starts, turns back, then turns back again. By burnishing the dowel, slight kinks like this can be pinpointed and removed. In order to burnish a shaft, you need an arrow-shaft burnisher. Really, anything that is hard, and with a nice polish will work. Having a rounded cross-section is a bonus, as this helps increase pressure. Stainless steel rods, glass jars, bone, plastic, and even other pieces of wood make good burnishers.

For really stubborn shafts, the end hole of a crescent wrench or similar hand tool can be used to pull out bends.

Arrow Shafts

Whichever way you go, the process is the same.

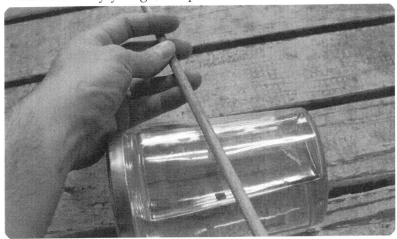

Take your dowel and run it over your burnisher, applying downward force against the kink. To exert more pressure, you can place the dowel on a semi-hard surface like a leg or a floor mat and press the burnisher into it. To burnish the surface, keep moving either the dowel or burnisher back and forth. The constant pressure and built up heat will help compress and straighten the fibers in the dowel, like the picture below.

If your dowel is especially troublesome and won't straighten up by the first two methods, heating it is the last resort. Heating also works for shafts that keep returning to their curved shape, no matter how many times they are straightened, like the dowel below. Because heating takes moisture from the wood, doing it too many times will cause the wood to become brittle. If you need to do it again, let the dowel rest in a cool humid place for a while.

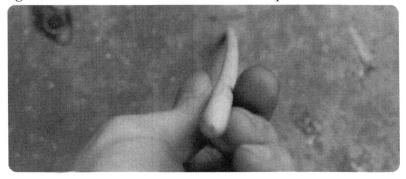

To start, you will need a source of dry heat. Your average household has a good one. Any stovetop, whether gas or electric, will work. A torch will work as well, though it may burn the shaft so be careful. A heat gun and some high-powered hair-dryers work as well.

Arrow Shafts

Carefully and quickly move the area to be bent over the heat source, or in the case of a heat gun, move the heat source over the dowel. Don't stay in one place too long, as it may burn the shaft or at least cause uneven bending.

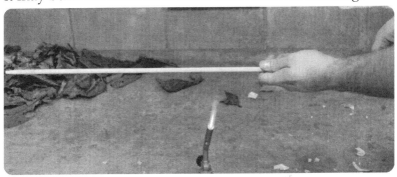

Keep moving the dowel over the heat source until it starts to droop very slightly. That will tell you the wood has become semi-plastic and will move.

Now simply straighten the shaft out like you would with any other, by hand. It helps to wear gloves or have a leather pad between you and dowel, as they can get very hot. Sadly, my hands are already used to it.

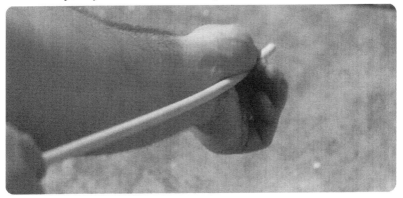

Once straightened, make sure that the dowel stays straight while cooling. Bundling it with some other shafts or even just watching it as it cools are good options. Once straightened, it should look something like this.

If the shaft has any kinks, go back and burnish it now. By using all three techniques together, you can straighten almost any dowel that comes your way. Now that you've got some straight shafts, we'll go over cresting and finishing.

Cresting

Cresting is simply painting your arrow so that it can be easily identified. Bright colors make a shaft easier to see in grass or foliage, and darker colors help break up the arrow's outline. Get creative.

There are cresting jigs that make this much easier. If and when I crest arrows, (I personally don't that often. I usually sign all my arrows) I usually do it all by hand. If you want to crest arrows with some level of ease and repeatability, a normal power-drill works wonders.

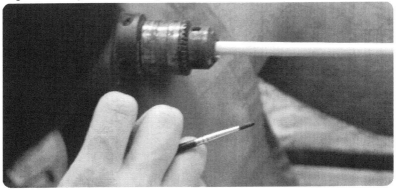

Simply chuck the nock end of the shaft into your drill. This is also a great way to test how straight your shafts are. If the shaft does not spin evenly, it still needs to be straightened. If the shaft does not spin true, the cresting will come out uneven and sloppy.

What I usually do is set the drill very slowly, and apply the lines with very light pressure, going over them a few times. When cresting, try and pick a pattern that appeals to you. Cresting was once popular when everyone shot wooden shafts. Nowadays, just having wood arrows distinguishes you from everyone else. Hopefully that will change again.

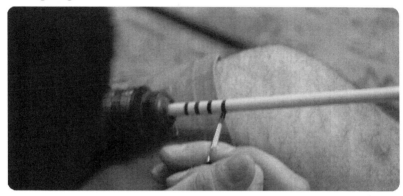

Once you've got your pattern down, you can copy it on other arrows. A set of crested arrows is quite impressive.

As you can see, it will take practice to make even cresting. Practicing on the scrap ends of dowels is a good place to start.

Finishing

When you've completed every other aspect of turning wooden dowels into arrow shafts, all that is left is finishing the shafts. While there are many ways of finishing and sealing an arrow shaft, my personal favorite for dowels is the simplest.

I coat the arrows in oil, usually boiled linseed oil, though almost anything will work. After a few coats of oil, I wipe off the excess and then burnish the shaft with a glass jar.

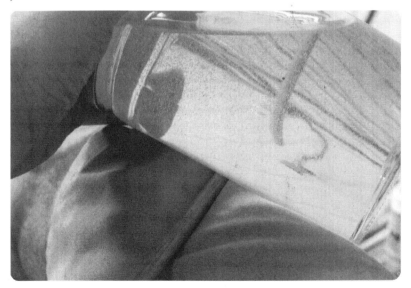

By burnishing the shaft, you not only get a nice, polished appearance, but you also strengthen the wood. Burnishing, unlike sanding or simply coating the wood with a sealer, compresses the outer layer of wood, making it more resistant to breakage. This compression helps keeps run-off from causing problems, as well as giving the arrow a high-gloss finish that only needs periodic oiling to keep it waterproof.

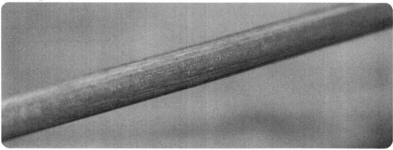

Burnishing is also easy to do, and requires no sanding or dry time. Another reason why I oil my arrows is because of the questionable moisture content or dowels. Simply sealing an already dry dowel will make it brittle. Oiling a dry dowel will give the wood some added elasticity, which is important for a flexing arrow in flight.

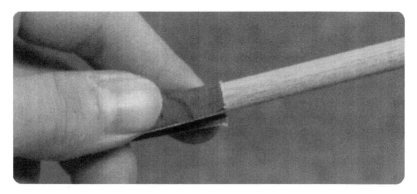

Alternatively, you could simply sand and oil your arrows. Sanding the arrow with ever-increasing grit will allow for a smooth surface that will resist breakage and splinters.

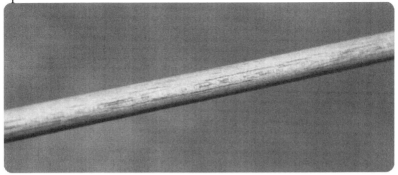

Then just finish the shaft with your choice of oil or sealer. You can also sand first, oil, then burnish the shafts for an extra-high gloss. Experiment and find what suits you best.

Chapter 2
All the Fixin's

Now that you've got your dowel arrow shafts, all you need to do is affix points, nocks, and put some feathers on them. And then viola! You have a finished arrow.

In this chapter, we'll go over fitting store bought tips and nocks onto your dowel shafts, making a tie-in broadhead for hunting larger game, a wooden blunt for small game, cutting a self nock, and finally how to do an easy to replace feather fletch.

With that said, let's get started!

Fitting Glue-On Components

One of the best ways to minimize other factors regarding the tuning of your arrows is to use factory made nocks and tips. Target and field points are fairly inexpensive, usually not more than 50 cents each. As for nocks, most plastic nocks are only a dollar or so for a dozen.

The benefit of using pre-made points is that each point is uniform. You can play with spine by buying different weights of point. Having uniform points also makes fitting replacements in the field a lot easier. Imagine having to re-file a nock or re-fit a home-made point. Most times, the shaft will be ruined anyway.

As for nocks, the plastic variety has many advantages. One, if the nock ever fails, chances are your arrow won't fail with it. Two, if you ever do lose a nock, another will easily fit into place quickly. Three, most plastic nocks snap onto the string, a good quality that may not be safe to have in a self nock. In my opinion, plastic nocks are a better choice for arrows that are going to be shot repeatedly. And the time you save is usually worth the money.

Most store-bought points and nocks are tapered

on the inside to fit onto a tapered shaft. The set angle of taper is 5 degrees for the tip and 10 degrees for the nock. Since the angle is fairly precise, I suggest buying an arrow tapering tool like the one on the last page. They are plastic and can be purchased online from 3 Rivers Archery or at most traditional archery shops. After trying to cut the tapers myself, this is by far the best $5 I've spent.

To use the taper tool, simply insert the arrow shaft and twist. it is exactly like using a hand-powered pencil sharpener.

This is what the 5 degree angle taper looks like on an arrow shaft. This will fit in all 5 degree taper points.

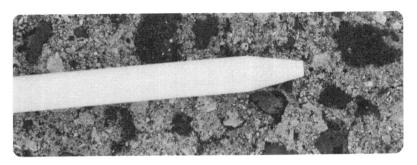

Here's what a 10 degree nock taper looks like. If using a taper tool on larger diameter shafts, the shaft will have to be filed and sanded until the tool fits.

My favorite adhesive for mounting points and nocks is hot melt glue. Simply heat up the end of a stick of hot glue, and smear some of it on the tapered ends.

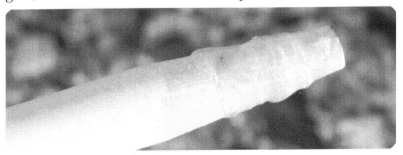

When attaching your point and nock, simply heat up the end of the shaft, melting the glue before attaching.

Glue on nocks and points come in many shapes and sizes. Pictured here is a white glue-on nock with an indexer and a 75 grain steel field point.

To install a target or field point, simply heat up the shaft to melt the glue, and push the point on.

Before we install the nock, take a good look down the arrow. Here you can see that there is some run off, going toward the tip.

Turning the arrow over, you can see that the run-off on this side is coming towards you. This side should be angled towards the bow and you hand, as the run-off is less likely to lift up.

Now that you've established where the run off is going, position the nock on the end so that when on the bow, the run-off is heading towards you on the side where it meets the bow and rest.

the Self Nock

The self nock is the oldest style of nock. In effect, all it really is is a slit cut at the end of the arrow that holds the arrows onto the string when shooting. Self nocks, with their elegant simplicity, make good nocks for primitive and traditional arrows.

While not the most reliable nock, a good self nock will hold up to the stresses of normal shooting. I like to shoot self-arrows when using my guava selfbow, as they seem to match each other in feel and spirit. These nocks are also perfect for Native American replica arrows, award arrows, and display arrows. There is just something about them that brings out that primal energy of our hunting ancestors.

This particular style of self nock is the most basic and quite durable. It does not lock on the string, and should not be used on compound bows, as the added force may cause it to split.

I have marked the end of an arrow for you to see the growth rings. Make sure to keep the rings running horizontally.

Start the nock off by creating a little groove with a file. Make sure it runs perpendicular to the growth rings, so that the nock is less likely to split.

To cut the nock, take three normal hacksaw blades and tape them together. This will give you roughly the size of a normal nock. For a tighter fit, only use two.

Make sure to keep the blades going in straight, or the nock will be crooked. Keep cutting until the back of the blades are flush to the end of the nock.

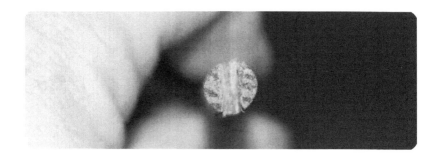

Once cut, make sure the nock is straight. If not, you can make minor adjustments with sandpaper.

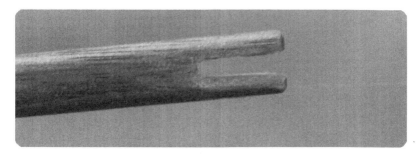

Here is the finished self nock. If you plan on gluing your feathers on, a little thread wrapped just below the nock will give it extra strength and help prevent splitting.

Traditional Steel Broadhead

While I stand by using precision parts for arrows, I do have to say that nothing looks more impressive than a nice handmade steel broadhead. While these are more than enough for large game, be sure to check your local laws regarding what types of broadheads you can use.

Here in Hawaii, the only stipulation is that the blade be at least $1^1/_4$″ wide. I use $1/_{16}$″ thick O1 tool steel, though even mild steel will sharpen up sufficiently and hold up under use. I've also had success using bedframe angle iron, which is a little under $1/_8$″ thick.

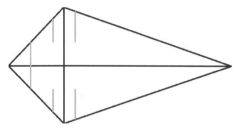

This little template above is my favorite type of hand-made broadhead. Its shape is based loosely on some glue-on broadheads that I use. It is to scale and can be copied as-is for use as a template. The dimensions are $2^1/_2$″ L x $1^1/_4$″ W. The little cross-line goes in at $1^7/_8$″ from the point. The three gray lines are each $1/_4$″ apart. The inner gray lines are separated by $1/_2$″ in the center. If copying by hand, your template should look like the one below.

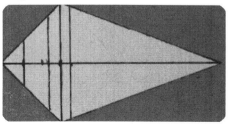

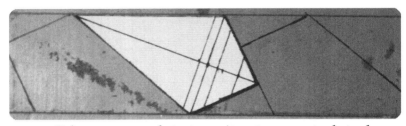

Take your template, trace it onto your steel stock, and cut your blanks out. A hacksaw works well for this.

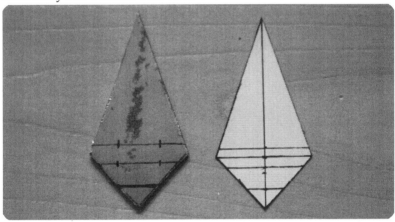

Once cut out, transfer the end and notch cut lines onto your blank.

All the Fixin's

Make sure that the lashing notches leave $\frac{1}{2}$" in the center. This gives the broadhead maximum stability while still allowing for a secure lashing. Also be sure to round off the inner sharp edges of the notches.

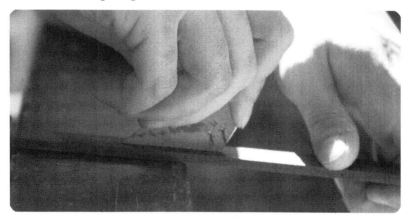

Using a file, grinder, or belt sander, flatten and true up all five sides of the broadhead blank. Make sure to keep the back flat, as this is the part that contacts the arrow.

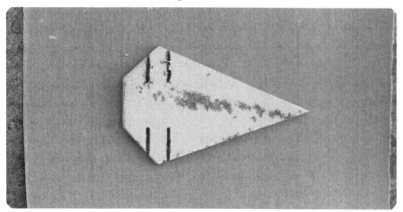

Once the edges are trued up, take a piece of 220-320 sandpaper and mooth up both faces. This will also rough up the steel for the next step.

51

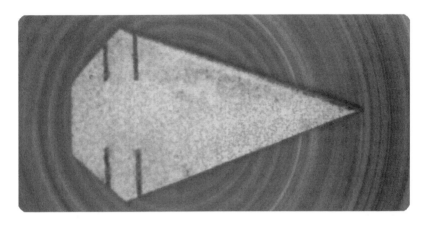

In order to protect the steel from rust slightly, take a small bowl and pour in enough vinegar to fill up about half an inch. Microwave it for a minute, being careful as it will be hot. Place your broadhead blank into the bowl. It should start to bubble. Once it does, flip the broadhead over.

Once the vinegar stops bubbling, remove the blank from the bowl and wash it with some dish soap to stop the acid. Pat it dry, then rub some mineral or vegetable oil on it to inhibit rust. Depending on the steel and strength of your vinegar, its color will range from light gray to black at this point.

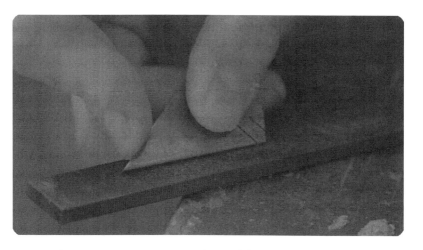

Begin creating your edge. I like about a 30 degree angle. This can be done on a file, or with a grinder or belt sander.

Once your bevel goes about halfway down the edge, flip the blank over and repeat on the opposite face. Do not completey sharpen the edge yet. That can be done on a file or stone before its first use.

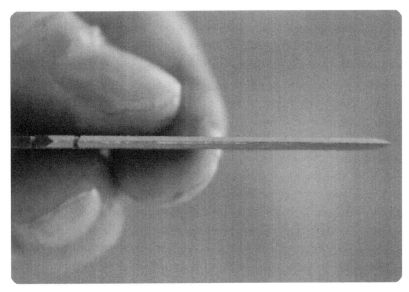

This is what your edge should look like. It should be even, but not fully-sharp yet.

Here is your finished broadhead, ready to be lashed onto an arrow.

-Hafting the Point

Unlike socketed, tapered points, the tie-in broadhead needs to be tied-in, as the name implies. This process is time-consuming, but needs to be done right to ensure that the arrow lives a long, healthy life and the tip doesn't simply break off of the arrow. Whenever you are dealing with life and death, you need to make sure that you do it properly and with respect.

I lash my points with artificial sinew though silk, nylon, and polyester threads all work well. If using cotton, linen, or hemp, be sure to soak the lashing with a waterproof wood glue prior to wrapping, as it will keep the fibers from weakening and coming apart.

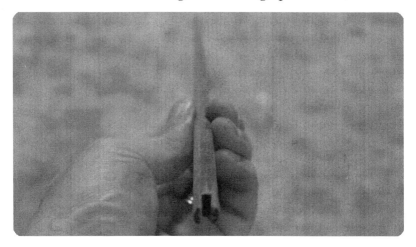

To figure out where your broadhead will go, start at the nock end with the string groove vertical. If mounting your broadhead horizontally, which is what I prefer, the slot for it will be cut perpendicular to the nock. If mounting vertically, the slot will be in line with the nock.

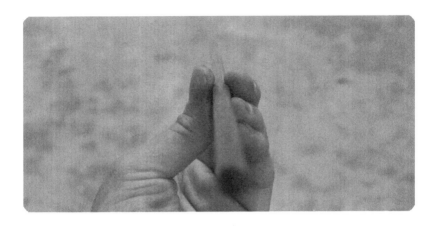

Go to the other end of the arrow, keeping in mind where the nock is in relation to this side. Check a couple times, to make sure you have this side lined up with the nock.

Once you have an idea of where the nock is, mark your broadhead slot. In the picture above, I am marking for a horizontal mounting.

To cut the slot for your broadhead, use two hacksaw blades for $\frac{1}{16}$", and three for $\frac{1}{8}$" thick broadheads.

Cut the slot down one inch, checking often for fit. Make sure to go straight into the arrow shaft. Once down to the bottom, make sure it is square, as this is where the broadhead contacts the arrow.

With a file or belt sander, smooth the end of the arrow down. You want this to be a nice, smooth transition. Not too thin, to keep the strength of the joint, but not too thick as the wood may get sheared off when the point hits its target.

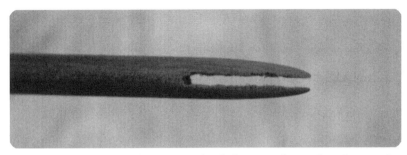

Once the end is smoothed down, clean the slot up in preparation for gluing.

Fill the slot with either hot glue or epoxy. If using hot glue, make sure to heat the glue up prior to inserting the point.

Once glued in, keep the tip secured and straight until the glue sets.

All the Fixin's

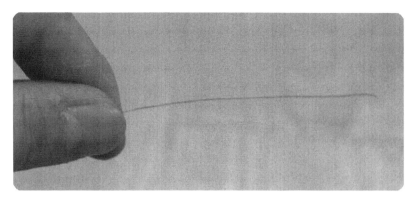

Get a five foot length of strong thread for lashing.

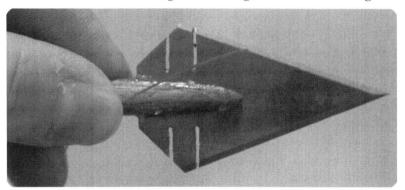

Place one end of the thread facing the tip of the arrow.

Start wrapping the long end over the short end toward the point.

59

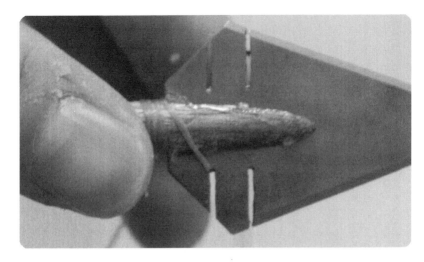

Once your wraps reach the bottom of the point, pull the short end of the thread tight, then back and out of the way. Take the long end and slip it into one of the lashing notches.

Wrap the long end around and into the next notch up.

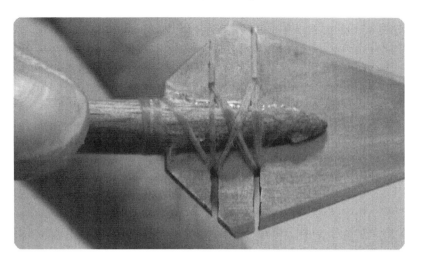

Wrap the thread across to the arrow shaft a few times, then wrap the thread throuhg the notches in a criss-cross pattern, ending up in the bottom notch.

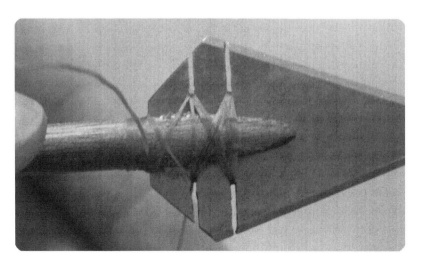

Keep wrapping, criss-crossing the thread between the bottom notch and the bottom of the point.

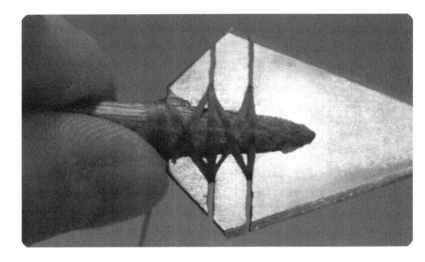

Once the bottom wrap matches the top wrap, start wrapping over the very first wrap you did on the arrow shaft.

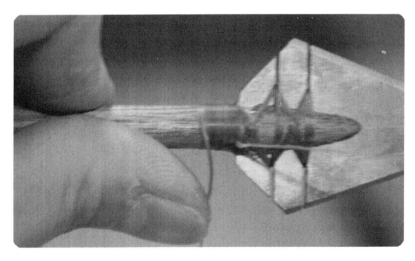

Continue wrapping for about $\frac{1}{4}''$, then turn the arrow around so it is easier to finish the wrap.

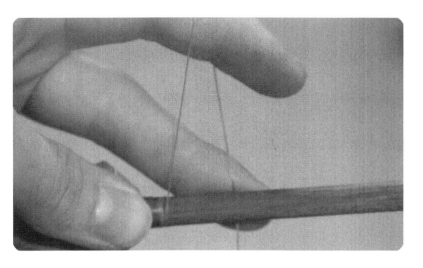

Hold the shaft with one hand, and lift your index finger. Wrap the thread over that finger, creating a loop. Keep the wrap going in the same direction.

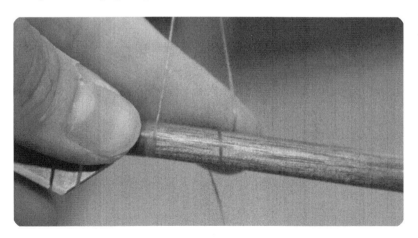

Now take the end of the thread and wrap it up and into the loop, effectively continuing the wrap in the same direction, but down towards the tip instead of towards the nock.

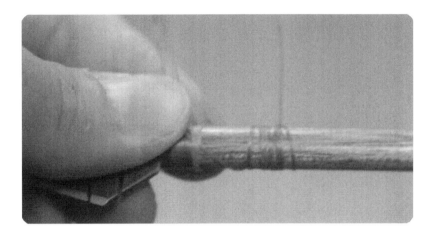

Keep wrapping on the inside of the loop for about $1/4''$. Then take the end of the thread and lay it down towards the tip under the loop. Now take the loop itself, and by winding the loop around the arrow, it will pick up the wrap you just did and transfer it to the bottom.

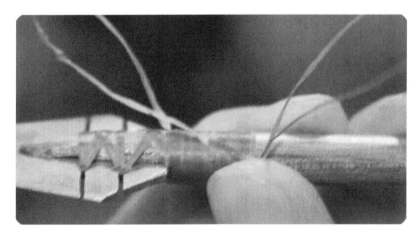

Once down to the end, pull on the loose end of the thread. That will tighten down the loop you make, tucking the end of the thread under itself.

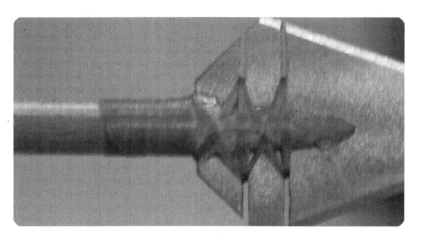

Once the ends are tightened, cut off the loose ends. A little bit of wood glue or epoxy wiped over the wrapping will help strengthen it and keep it waterproof.

Now that the point is lashed on, you can sharpen it up and you are ready to go. While a file usually works fine, a really sharp edge can be made by either using sharpening stones or some sandpaper on a flat surface.

Wood Blunt

In addition to making arrow shafts from dowels, you can also use them to make wooden blunt points. These wooden blunts are good for stunning small game; whereas a sharpened point would go right through, merely injuring an animal.

While not as durable as their rubber and steel counterparts, wooden blunts still pack a punch. $3/4''$ wooden dowels work great for this purpose. Pick the heavier species like maple and oak. If you want a good stump-shooting arrow, lignum vitae and ipe are practically indestructable.

These blunts are good to make in large quantities as they may break with use, but can be easily removed and replaced. These blunts can also be slipped over most target points (this works best if a little padding is pushed in first), and can also be used to extend the life of an arrow with a broken tip.

The easiest way to make these blunts is with a woodturning lathe. I wouldn't suggest getting a lathe just for making these, but if you don't have one, chances are someone in your area does. Ask around. Some community centers have public workshops, and some universities will let you use their equipment if you ask.

If you don't have access to a lathe or wish to do without, a simple power drill and a wood rasp is all you need.

If using a lathe, you will need a drill chuck that fits into the headstock. These are fairly inexpensive, and some old drill-press chucks will fit in a lathe. You can also use a power drill instead of a lathe. On top of those, you will also need a 3 inch long piece of dowel the same diameter as your arrows to serve as a mandrel.

For the actual blunt, cut a piece of $3/_4$" dowel 2 inches long. Maple is a good choice.

67

Mark the center. One way to do this is to mark straight lines across the face of the dowel.

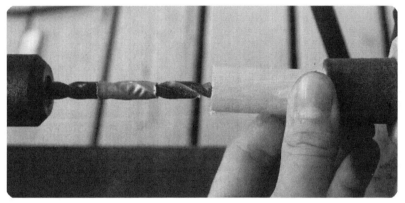

If using a lathe, hold the dowel in the tailstock and drill a hole equal to your arrow-diameter to a depth of 1 inch.

Once the hole is drilled, insert the 3 inch long dowel into the end.

Chuck the mandrel in the lathe.

Cut the dowel down to this shape. You want the end to be flat-faced but rounded slightly at the edges, and it should have a slight curve going back to prevent splitting.

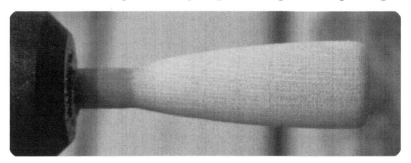

After roughing the shape, sand the tip until it is smooth. You can also finish it on the lathe with wax or lathe-applied finish of choice.

Now the blunt is ready for attaching.

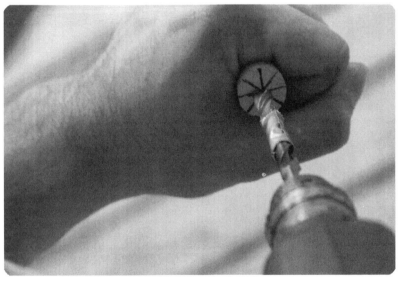

If using a hand drill, hold or clamp the dowel and drill a one inch deep hole.

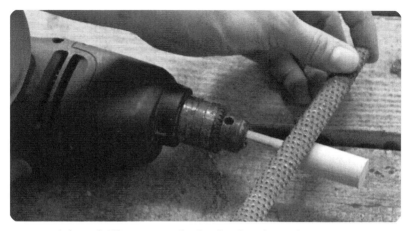

After drilling your hole, fit the dowel onto the mandrel and insert it into the drill. Either lock the drill on and press a rasp into it, or clamp the rasp down and push the drill into it.

Rasp the dowel down to this rough shape. Leave it a little large, as the rasp leaves very rough edges.

Sand the dowel down and apply the finish of your choice.

Your wooden blunt is finished and ready for attaching. Using a lathe and drill press, I can usually make a batch of a few dozen in an hour or so. With a hand drill, I can make a few in an hour. Either way, they are fairly easy to make, so make a bunch and keep some on hand.

-Fitting the Tip

Because these blunts are really just wooden sleeves, they are very easy to install. If you don't want to, you don't even need to glue them. Just adding a bit of hot glue to the very tip, or inserting a piece of neoprene will help keep the point from splitting.

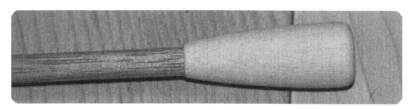

Test-fit to see if the blunt fits over your arrow. You could just leave it as is.

For a more permanent point, smear some hot glue over the arrow, scraping a large blob onto the tip for extra cushion.

Heat the glue on the arrow, then slip the blunt over the tip. Remove the excess glue and you are ready to go.

Fletching

Fletching is the vital finishing touch on any arrow. Call it the spark of life, if you will. Without it, an arrow is just a stick, but with it the arrow has direction and stability. Mastering the art of fletching, especially by hand, is a long and arduous process. It takes much practice to be able to affix feathers onto an arrow properly.

I have spent hour upon hour perfecting my fletching skills, gluing each feather to the shaft individually. While very pretty and impressive in its own right, my fletching had one quality I didn't like: it was stuck there.

Might sound counter-intuitive, but my cautious outlook on arrows has led me to a mindset of trying to salvage what I can. If a shaft ever broke, I had a perfect fletch on a broken arrow. If the feathers wore out, I would have to scrape them off, ruining the finish of my arrow.

Eventually I looked back to early man, and found a simple and effective method of affixing feather to a shaft. By taking a length of thread, one can basically lash feathers onto an arrow. This gives three big advantages.

One, the feathers can be adjusted after attatchment, allowing even the inexperienced to make accurate fletchings. Two, this method of fletching can be done with little prep-work, and even works on un-ground, split feathers. Three, since the feathers aren't glued, they can be removed easily. Now if a shaft breaks or feathers wear out, take the feathers off.

Start with five feet of thread. Artificial sinew and waxed dacron have become my favorites.

Take one of your feathers and measure so that there is an inch of space between feather and the notch of the nock. Start your wrap $^1/_4''$ below the feather.

Hold the short end against the arrow towards the nock, and wrap $^1/_4''$ on top of the short end.

Once you've wrapped $1/4$", pull the short end tight and move it back and out of the way.

Before placing the first feather, look down the shaft. See how the run-off points away from you? This is the side you want to put your first feather.

Tuck the front end of the first feather into the wrap slightly, then wrap the string over to keep it in place. This will be your odd feather.

At about $^1/_3$ of the arrow's circumfrence away, place your second feather.

And again for the third feather.

From the back, this is what your feathers should look like.

Once your feathers are on, secure them in place by tightly wrapping the first $^1/_8$" of the feathers with your thread.

Start wrapping into the feathers. Simply take your thread and place it into the feather. It will separate.

One wrap per $\frac{1}{4}$" is good. Any less and the feathers will be too loose. Any more, and the feathers may get too ruffled.

Wrap the last $\frac{1}{8}$" of feathers to secure the back end.

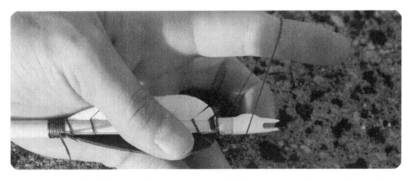

To finish up the wrap, hold the arrow in one hand and lift your index finger. Make a loop like this.

All the Fixin's

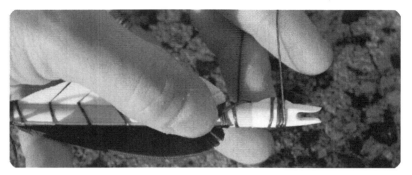

Take the end of your thread and pass it through the loop, as if you are wrapping the shaft backwards, but in the same rotation. If you wrapped the feather clockwise, keep wrapping clockwise.

Tuck the short end under the loop, then rotate the loop around the arrow, transferring the wrap from the top to the bottom.

Once the wrap is done, pull the end tight to secure it.

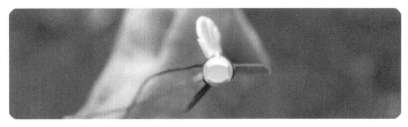

The feathers will probably be crooked. The beauty of wrapping the feathers is that you can fix this easily.

Gently push the feathers around with a fingernail until all three feather line up like in this picture.

And now you have a fletched arrow. It is all finished and ready to shoot!

Chapter 3
Putting it All Together

Now that you know how to go from dowel to arrow shaft, have a good idea of how to put points, nocks, and feathers onto your arrows, it's time to put it all together.

This chapter is more of a quick overview in relation to building arrows. We will go through the basic construction of five different arrows, each one referring back to steps previously outlined in this book.

This section is mainly for you to get ideas for your own arrow creations. We will be building a target arrow and hunting arrow with glue on components. We will also be building a blunt arrow with glue on nock, as well as a more prmitive looking self-nock blunt arrow. To finish it all off, we will be making a hunting self arrow with a tie in broadhead.

All of these arrows are made for a 45-55 pound bow. The target and blunt arrows are cut to 30 inches, the two broadhead arrows are cut to 32. These are some good starter arrows to base your own off of. Go on, get creative, it's your time to shine!

Alright, let's get to it!

Target Arrow

This little arrow is about as basic as you can get. It is fitted with 75 grain field points and 3 inch feathers. These are great for target shooting, and with glue on nocks and points, there is almost nothing to them.

Start by cutting a 30" arrow shaft.

Taper the ends and glue on the tip and nock.

Fletch the arrow.

Here is the completed target arrow, ready to shoot.

Hunting Arrow

When it comes to broadheads, there are a plethora of different brands and styles of point. You have 2-blade, 3-blade, 4-blade, and even more variations. The broadhead here is a Magnus 2 blade, 110 grain, and is mounted horizontally.

Cut your arrow shaft to 32". It should be fairly stiff.

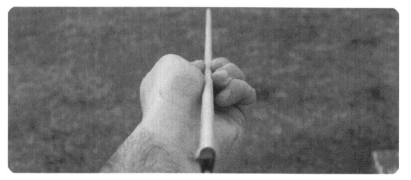

To line up the tip, hold the nock notch vertical...

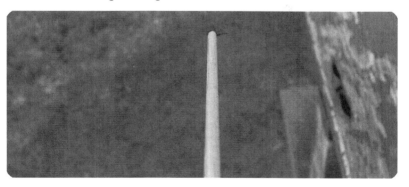

and affix the tip horizontally.

While the glue is still setting, make sure the tip is lined up straight.

Fletch your arrow. Orange and neon yellow are my favorite fletchings to use for hunting.

Here is the finished hunting arrow. Tune it and sharpen the tip, and you are ready to go.

Blunt Arrow

This little blunt arrow is almost the same as the target arrow except it has a wooden blunt glued to the end instead of a field point. These make great small game arrows or for shooting into grass.

Cut your arrow shaft 30″ long.

Glue the nock and blunt tip onto the shaft.

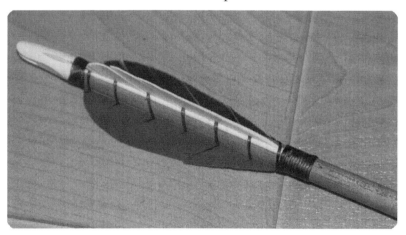

Fletch your arrow.

Here is the finished blunt arrow.

Traditional Blunt Arrow

With a self nock and shortened feathers, this arrow looks quite primitive. Combine that with a wooden blunt and you have an impressive little stump shooter.

Start with a 30″ arrow shaft plus $\frac{1}{4}$″ to make up for the self nock.

Glue the blunt in place and cut your self nock. Make sure to go across the growth rings when cutting the self nock.

This blunt arrow is inspired by a Native American bird arrow. While not an exact replica of any one tribe or nation, this arrow draws its unique appearance from the feathers used.

Most Native American arrows were cut from full-feathers, and so the fletchings reflect the feather simply being cut on the front and back. This style gives a distinct type of fletching that just screams, "I'm an Arrow!"

Start with a five inch-parabolic feather, and cut an inch off of each end. This style of fletching works well for full split feathers, as well as whole feathers. Just treat each feather as you would a pre-cut feather.

Putting it All Together

Fletch the arrow an inch from the bottom of the nock. This gives a little bit of room for the fingers, while touching feather. If you don't want to touch feather, measure an inch from the furthest tips of the feathers.

Here is the finished traditional blunt arrow. This arrow makes a great display piece, as well as a practical arrow in its own right for hunting or stump-shooting.

Traditional Hunting Arrow

My personal favorite arrow, the Traditional Hunting Arrow, combines a self nock, a steel tie-in broadhead, five inch barred feathers, and a kwila shaft into a beautiful and deadly arrow. It is perfect for the selfbow hunter.

Start with a 32", stiff arrow shaft.

Cut the nock and lash your point.

Fletch your arrow. For self nocks, wrap a little more on the end to prevent splitting.

Here is the completed traditional hunting arrow. Just tune it and sharpen it up, and you are ready to go!

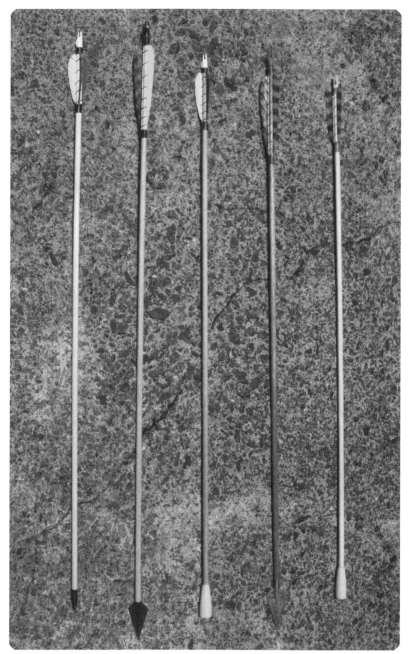

Chapter §
Bonus Track

Welcome to the Bonus Track! Now if you've ever met me, you would probably think I was a pretty neat guy, if perhaps a little strange. Then it should come as no suprise that even though I am a bowyer and I love my selfbows, I also shoot a compound (I hear it's ancient. Come on, it's at least thirty years younger than my favorite recurve!) bow.

Now, I have often wondered if there was a better way. If I could have the benefits of my wooden arrows and still have the modern features of a modern arrow. Don't worry, you will be assimilated. Resistance is futile.

the Cyborg

Ah, the cyborg. A blend of organic and mechanic, the fusion of the natural and the synthetic. I used to have some nice aluminum hunting arrows. After all the vanes stripped off and the nocks fell out, I retired them.

Now that I have some nice aluminum tubes, I had the brilliant idea of trying to breathe some life into that dead metal. If I took a wood shaft and somehow attached some of the aluminum shaft to the front like a footed arrow, I could have a wooden arrow with interchangeable tips!

It would also represent my embrace of both the modern and the primitive. Without further ado, I present the Cyborg.

I started with my 2216 (that's the sizing for aluminum arrows) aluminum arrow shaft, a $3/8$" dowel shaft, and a scrap $5/16$" dowel. The 2216 is roughly $11/32$".

Cut the dowel shaft down to 29", the aluminum shaft down to 6", and the little dowel down to 2". This is more or less how it will all fit together.

The $5/16$" dowel fits perfectly snug inside the aluminum shaft. If there is some play, a little duct tape wrapped around will take care of that.

Once you've pushed the dowel in as far as you can, take another dowel and mark an inch on it. Tapering the end makes it easier to push into the aluminum. Take this dowel and drive the 2"dowel in one inch. This should give enough space for any basic insert and screw-in points.

Take another dowel and measure the exact depth of the opposite side, so you know how much you need to cut on your dowel arrow shaft.

Use the mark on that dowel to transfer the depth to your arrow shaft. Put the dowel shaft on the side for now.

Mark two inches in from the short side of the aluminum fore-shaft. This should place it right in the middle of the wooden dowel that's inside.

Either take a nail and drive it through this spot, or drill a hole and run a nail or soft steel or copper wire through.

Cut the nail about $1/_8$" on both sides, the hammer it down until it the ends expand, locking the nail in place.

With a file, bring the ends of the nail down flush with the fore-shaft so it won't catch or snag on anything when fired.

Now go back to the dowel shaft and cut a $5/_{16}$" tenon. You want a nice, square-shouldered base that the fore-shaft can sit on.

Test-fit the fore-shaft. Once it fits well, remove it and sand the end of the dowel shaft so that transition from wood to metal is smooth.

Once everything is nice and smooth, glue the foreshaft onto the dowel arrow shaft.

Since the aluminum arrow I am using had its tip nocked out after hitting a rock, I had to get a new insert. You could also just use the front end of an arrow that still has its insert. I am also using a $^{11}/_{32}$" glue-on nock.

Glue in the insert and fit the nock on. If using a $^{11}/_{32}$" taper tool, the and of the arrow will need to be filed and sanded to a taper to fit. If using a $^{23}/_{64}$" taper tool, only a light sanding is needed, if that. ($^3/_8$" is $^{24}/_{64}$")

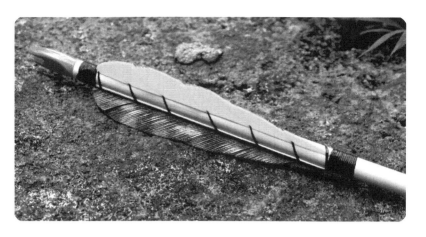

Fletch the arrow with the feathers of your choice.

Congratulations! You have your very own cyborg arrow. You no longer have to choose between a target, hunting, or stump-shooting arrow! You now have them all-in-one! As a side note, this arrow is extremely tip-heavy so I suggest using the lightest points available.

Well, that's it for the bonus track. If you want more arrow stuff, go back to the beginning. If you want to build your own basic bow, check out <u>the Backyard Bowyer : the Beginner's Guide to Building Bows</u>.

11279660R00056